D1528839

Exploring Physical Science

Exploring

ELECTRICITY
AND
MAGNETISM

Andrew Solway

New York

537 Solway

Published in 2008 by The Rosen Publishing Group, Inc.
29 East 21st Street, New York, NY 10010

Copyright © 2008 Wayland/The Rosen Publishing Group, Inc.

First Edition

Cover photograph: Daniel Brunner/istockphoto.com

Photo credits: P. 4: Allen Johnson/istockphoto.com; p. 5: Lester Lefkowitz/Getty Images;
p. 6: Frank Podgorsek; p. 8: Hulton Archive/Getty Images; p. 10: Mansell/Time Life Pictures/
Getty Images; p. 12: Honda UK; p. 13: NASA; p. 14: Philips; p. 16: Baldur Tryggvason/
istockphoto.com; p. 17: Joe Gough/istockphoto.com; p. 18: istockphoto.com; p. 19: Charles
Neal/istockphoto.com; p. 21: Bobbie Osborne/istockphoto.com; p. 22: AVTG/istockphoto.com;
p. 23: Chris Fairclough/cfwimages.com; p. 24: Sean Locke/ istockphoto.com; p. 25: Discovery
Media; p. 27: Thomas Mounsey/istockphoto.com; p. 28: Tom Laloo/istockphoto.com; p.29:
Falk Kienas/istockphoto.com; p. 30: Thomas Hottner/istockphoto.com; p. 32: Andrew Lambert
Photography/Science Photo Library; p. 33: NRM Pictorial Collection/Science and Society
Picture Library; p. 36: PDL Design/ istockphoto.com; p. 39: Hulton Archive/Getty Images;
p. 40: Ed Parker/EASI-Images/ cfwimages.com; p. 41: Honda UK; p. 42: Fox Photos/Getty
Images; p. 43: Keystone/Getty Images; p. 44: Martin Bond/Science Photo Library; p. 45:
Cambridge Display Technology

Library of Congress Cataloging-in-Publication Data

Saunders, N. (Nigel)
  Electricity and magnetism / Nigel Saunders. -- 1st ed.
      p. cm. -- (Exploring Physical Science)
  Includes index.
  ISBN-13: 978-1-4042-3749-0 (library binding)
  ISBN-10: 1-4042-3749-6 (library binding)
  1. Electricity--Juvenile literature. 2. Magnetism--Juvenile literature. I. Title.
  QC527.2.S38 2007
  537--dc22
                        2006039191

Manufactured in China

Contents

1 A powerful force 4

2 Charged or flowing 6

3 Circuits and batteries 14

4 Household power supply 22

5 Magnetic attraction 26

6 Magnetic electricity 30

7 Energy for electricity 36

8 Electric past and future 42

Glossary 46

Further information 47

Index 48

CHAPTER I

A powerful force

Electricity is probably the most important form of energy in the modern world. Energy is the ability to make things happen, and electricity makes plenty of things happen. Today, it powers everything from electric lights to space probes. Electric energy usually flows through wires, but scientists have shown that electric charge is a natural property of all substances. It is found within the **atoms** that make up everything in the universe.

Lightning energy

On a stormy night, a jagged bolt of lightning cuts across the sky with a tremendous ripping sound. The power of a lightning bolt is awesome—it can split a tree in half as easily as a knife cuts through butter.

Lightning is the most spectacular natural demonstration of electricity. Lightning is caused by a buildup of charge, or static electricity. In this book we will explore static electricity, and find out how scientists learned more about lightning from one of the most dangerous electrical experiments ever. We will also look at electricity flowing in circuits, at how power stations generate electricity, and at some ways we might use electricity in the future.

Lightning is the most dramatic kind of natural electricity. A lightning bolt is a giant spark between the clouds and Earth.

Magnetism

This book also looks at magnetism and electromagnetism. **Magnetism** is a force of attraction or repulsion that can act between two objects. Like electricity, magnetism is a natural force that originates in atoms, but we see magnetic effects only in iron and a few other magnetic substances. Magnetism and electricity are closely related. Some of our most useful electrical devices rely on a combination of electricity with magnetism to make them work.

In the past, magnetic forces were treated as a form of magic. Today, scientists understand much more about magnetism, and have found new ways to apply it. We can use magnetism to find our way around the world, to produce electricity, and to levitate objects off the ground.

So let's start at the beginning, with the first kind of electricity to be discovered—static electricity.

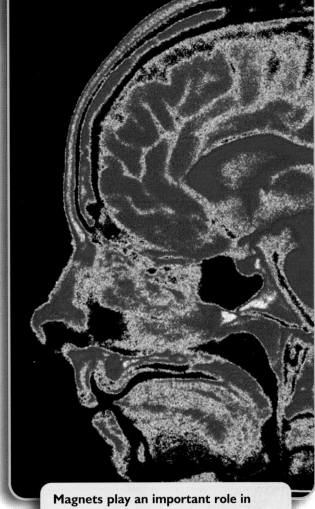

Magnets play an important role in modern medicine. Magnetic resonance imaging (MRI) scanners use a combination of strong magnets and radio waves to produce clear images of the body's internal structures.

AMAZING FACTS

Living electricity

People and other animals rely on electricity to control their bodies. The millions of messages that flash around our brain and travel along our nerves every minute of the day are carried by electricity.

CHAPTER 2

Charged or flowing

Static electricity

Static electricity is a buildup of electric charge. When certain substances are rubbed together, one of them becomes positively charged and the other becomes negatively charged. An object with an electric charge attracts anything with either an opposite electric charge, or no electric charge. You can very easily see how this works. Take a balloon, blow it up, and rub it against a woolen sweater or other piece of wool. As you rub, the balloon gets a negative charge and the jumper becomes positively charged. Now take the balloon and press it lightly against a smooth wall. The balloon will stick to the wall, held there by its electric charge.

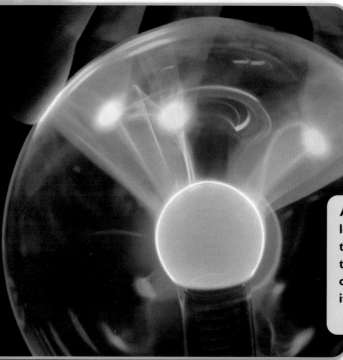

A plasma globe is a sphere full of gas at low pressure. In the center is a metal ball that can be charged with electricity. When the metal ball is charged up, electric charge travels from the ball to the glass. As it does so, it leaves trails of light in the gas.

 AMAZING FACTS

Attractive amber

The earliest discoveries about electricity were made in the sixth century B.C. The Greek philosopher, Thales of Miletus, found that if he rubbed a piece of amber with a soft cloth, the amber would attract light objects. This happened because rubbing charged the amber with static electricity.

Objects with the same electric charge repel (push away from) each other. You can check this out with another balloon experiment. This time charge two balloons, and tie them both to the same piece of string. Now hang the balloons over a stick, so that they both hang at the same level. Instead of touching, the balloons will repel each other and there will be a space between them.

What is charge?

Although scientists of the eighteenth and nineteenth centuries understood the properties of static electricity, they did not know what caused electric charge. The explanation came in the early 1900s, when scientists began to uncover the structure of atoms.

Every substance is made up of tiny particles called **atoms**. Each atom is made from even smaller particles known as **protons**, **neutrons**, and **electrons**. Protons and neutrons together make the **nucleus**, in the center of the atom. This has a positive electric charge. Around the nucleus is a cloud of tiny electrons, which are negatively charged. These electrons are responsible for producing electric charge.

When two substances come into contact, electrons on the surface transfer from one substance to the other. Some materials (such as the plastic that balloons are made from) tend to pick up electrons, and they become negatively charged. Others (such as wool) tend to lose electrons, and they become positively charged.

In an atom, there are the same number of protons as electrons, so that overall, the atom has no charge. This atom of the metal beryllium has four protons in the nucleus surrounded by four electrons.

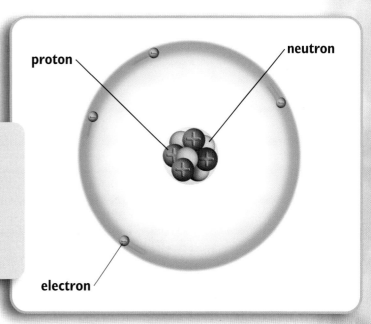

proton

neutron

electron

7

Losing charge

Something that is charged with electricity doesn't stay charged forever. Small specks of dust or tiny water droplets in the air can become charged themselves if they land on a charged object. Since they pick up the same charge as the object, they are then repelled from it. They float away, carrying with them a small amount of charge. If this happens over a period of time, the object slowly loses its charge.

GREAT EXPERIMENTS

Franklin's lightning experiment

In 1752, Benjamin Franklin showed that lightning was a huge electric spark caused by static buildup in the clouds. When a storm approached one day, he flew a kite with a metal spike on top of it. The kite string was wet, which meant it could conduct electricity down to a metal key on the string. Beyond the key, Franklin controlled the kite with a dry silk ribbon, which did not conduct electricity. The spike on the kite attracted electrical charge from the storm clouds. This electricity flowed down the wet string into the key. Franklin tested that there was electricity in the key by putting his knuckle near it, which produced sparks.

Franklin conducted his experiment safely, but he was incredibly lucky. The metal spike could have attracted a lightning strike, which would have killed Franklin.

Benjamin Franklin conducting his kite experiment.

Another way that an object can lose its charge is by touching a metal object that is "earthed" (connected to the ground). Metals cannot become charged, because they are electrical **conductors** (charge can pass through them). If a metal object touches something that is charged, the charge flows through the metal and into the ground.

Making sparks

If a charged object gets close to a piece of metal, a spark may pass between them. A spark is electricity "jumping" through the air between two objects. Air is not a good conductor, so sparks usually travel just a short distance through the air.

Following his kite experiment, Franklin invented the lightning rod. A lightning rod stops a building from being damaged by lightning. It is a metal spike high on top of the building, which is connnected by a wire into the ground. Any lightning near the building is attracted to the spike and is harmlessly **discharged** into the ground.

Making a current

Before the nineteenth century, the only way to make electricity was to collect electrical charge and then release it. This only produced electricity in short bursts. Then, in 1800, Alessandro Volta invented the first battery (see box). Batteries could supply a steady flow of electricity, called an **electric current**. A current is moving electricity, or in other words, it is a flow of electric charge (**electrons**).

GREAT SCIENTISTS

Alessandro Volta, 1745–1827

Alessandro Volta was born into a noble family in Como, Italy. He studied physics at school, and then at a university. In 1779, he became a professor of physics at Pavia University.

The following year, Volta's friend, Luigi Galvani, discovered that if two different metals were brought into contact with a muscle from a frog, an electric current was produced. Galvani thought that the current was caused by the frog muscle, but Volta was not convinced. He conducted a series of experiments, placing other materials between the metals. He found that cardboard soaked in a salt solution worked as well as frog muscle. In 1800, Volta used his discoveries to make a battery. It was a pile of copper and zinc disk, separated by disks of wet cardboard. This early kind of battery was called a **voltaic pile**.

Batteries make electricity through chemical reactions. In any battery there are two ends, or poles, one positive and one negative. The poles are known as **electrodes**. They are separated by another material known as an **electrolyte**. When the battery is connected, chemical reactions happen between the electrolyte and the electrodes. The chemical reaction that happens at the negative electrode produces electrons (negative electric charge). The chemical reaction at the positive electrode uses up electrons to produce a positive electric charge.

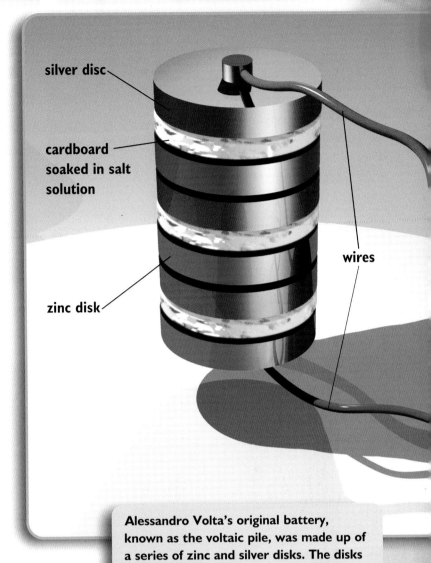

silver disc

cardboard soaked in salt solution

zinc disk

wires

Alessandro Volta's original battery, known as the voltaic pile, was made up of a series of zinc and silver disks. The disks were separated by pieces of cardboard soaked in salt solution.

Conductors and insulators

Electricity can only flow through electrical **conductors**—substances that allow electric charge to move through them. Metals are conductors because some of the electrons in a metal are not strongly bound to particular **atoms**—they form an electron "sea" around the metal atoms. These free-floating electrons can move to produce an electric current.

Materials that cannot carry an electric current are called electrical **insulators**. In an insulator, all the electrons are bound tightly to specific atoms, so they cannot move around freely.

Different batteries

The first battery was developed by Alessandro Volta in 1800. Volta's "voltaic pile" was not a single "battery," it was a whole series, piled one on top of another. Just one "battery," with one positive pole and one negative pole, is called an **electrical cell**. There are many different kinds of electrical cells. The metals that the **electrodes** are made from, and the chemicals used in the cell, affect properties, such as how powerful the battery is and how long it will last. Different kinds of cells and batteries are useful for different purposes. **Alkaline** cells are the type of batteries most often used in flashlights, portable radios, and other electric devices. Cameras and other devices that need sudden surges of power use lithium cells (**lithium** is a type of light metal). Lead-acid car batteries really are batteries, because they contain several cells joined together. They are powerful, tough batteries that can be recharged easily. The tiny button cells in watches and other small devices are made from silver oxide and zinc.

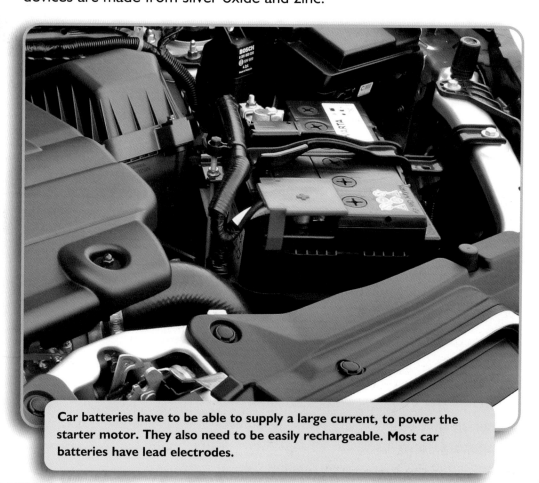

Car batteries have to be able to supply a large current, to power the starter motor. They also need to be easily rechargeable. Most car batteries have lead electrodes.

AMAZING FACTS

Nuclear-powered batteries

Long-distance space probes often run on solar power, using large solar panels to recharge their batteries. However, space probes that travel far out into the Solar System cannot get power this way, because the light from the Sun becomes too weak. The space probes *Voyager I* and *Voyager II* got around this problem by using **nuclear-powered** batteries. Some kinds of **semiconductor** material produce an electric current if one side is heated while the other is cooled. **Radioactive** materials, such as plutonium, naturally produce heat, and they can continue doing so for many years.

In a **nuclear-powered battery**, one side of an electricity-producing semiconductor is heated using a radioactive material, and this makes the semiconductor produce an electric current. The batteries in the *Voyager* space probes have lasted over 30 years, and are expected to last another 30 years.

The two *Voyager* space probes have now flown past Jupiter, Saturn, Uranus, and Neptune. They are still sending radio signals from beyond the Solar System.

One-use or rechargeable?

Batteries do not last forever. The reactions taking place inside gradually use up the battery's chemicals. Once they have gone flat, alkaline and other "one-use" batteries are dead and cannot be used again. However, many types of battery are rechargeable. If electric charge is pumped into a rechargeable battery, the chemical reactions in the battery go into reverse, and the battery charges up again.

CHAPTER 3

Circuits and batteries

You can use a battery to power your MP3 player or your bike lights. But they won't work unless they are connected correctly. The current has to flow in a loop from one pole of the battery to the other. This is called a **circuit**.

The simplest circuit

The simplest circuit you can make uses one **electrical cell**, two wires, and one electrical **component**—let's say a bulb. Connect one wire from the positive end of the battery to one side of the device, and the other wire from the negative end of the battery to the other end of the device. This connection will light the bulb.

This MP3 player contains some complex electronic circuitry. However, no matter how complex the circuit gets, the current still flows from one end of the battery, through the circuit, and back to the other end of the battery.

One problem with this simple circuit is that you have to keep connecting and disconnecting wires to turn the bulb on and off. An easier way to control this or any other circuit is to use a switch. When a switch is opened, it makes a break in the circuit and turns the power off. Closing the switch reconnects the circuit and allows electricity to flow.

Adding components

Only the simplest electrical devices—such as a bike light—have just one component (in this case the bulb) and one switch. Most other electrical devices have more components. In a complex electronic device such as a TV or a computer, there can be hundreds—or even thousands—of components. But even in the most complex circuit, the same basic rules apply—there must be a conducting path connecting one end of the battery to the other. Without such a path, the device will not work.

CIRCUIT SYMBOLS

Drawing an electrical circuit makes it easy to see and check all the connections, and to plan how it will work. When engineers draw circuits, they use special symbols to represent the different parts of the circuit. Some of the more common symbols are shown in the table below.

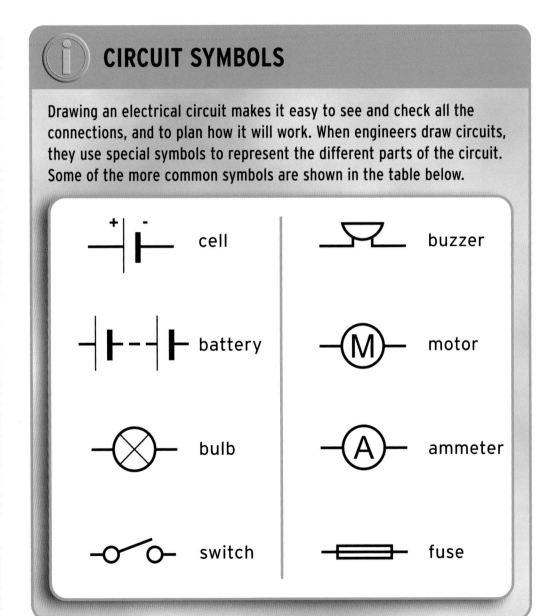

cell	buzzer
battery	motor
bulb	ammeter
switch	fuse

Flowing current

When you switch on an electric device, current instantly begins to flow in all parts of the circuit. One way to understand this is to think of the circuit as being like the chain on a bicycle. The "**component**" being operated by the chain is the back wheel, which turns as the chain goes around. The "battery" (the power that moves the chain, and therefore the wheel) is your legs as you press on the pedals. The "current" is the movement of the chain. As soon as you start pedaling, all parts of the chain begin to move.

A battery's "push"

We have seen that the current flow is the way that energy is transmitted to bulbs, motors, or other components of a circuit. It is the transmission system, like the chain on a bicycle. The energy to make the components work comes from the "push" of the battery—what we call its **voltage**. A battery with a large voltage can push more current around the circuit than one with a small voltage. The cells (batteries) commonly used are 1.5 volts. Household power supply is 110 volts in the United States and 230–240 volts in Europe.

The chain on a bicycle is like the electric current in a circuit. It carries energy from the "battery" (the cyclist's legs) to drive the "component" (the back wheel).

If we think about the bicycle idea again, the voltage of a battery is like the push of your legs on the pedals. If you are feeling tired and weak, your push will only make the chain go around slowly. But if you have been in training and are feeling fit, you will pedal faster and the chain will whirl around.

Pylons coming from a power station carry electricity at a very high voltage—up to half a million volts.

GREAT SCIENTISTS

André-Marie Ampère (1775–1836)

From a very young age, André-Marie Ampère had a thirst for knowledge. He began to do math problems with biscuit crumbs and pebbles, before he even knew how to write numbers. His main interest was in mathematics, but he also studied all the other sciences, languages, and poetry. Ampère is best known for his studies on electricity and magnetism, and the connections between them (see page 30). The unit for measuring current flow is named the **ampere** (amp) after him.

Resisting the flow

To make a circuit work, there must be a
component of some kind in it. A short circuit
is created when the ends of a battery are
simply connected together with a wire. A large
amount of current flows through the wire,
using up a lot of energy in a short time.

Having one or more components in a circuit adds
some resistance—something for the battery to "push against."
The resistance in a circuit depends on the number of components and
what type they are. Let's say, for instance, that we have a circuit with
two cells and a single bulb. The cells push a high current through the
circuit, which makes the bulb glow brightly. If we then add another bulb
in line with the first one, the resistance of the circuit is doubled. A higher
resistance means that less current flows through the circuit. Each bulb
gets less current, so the bulbs glow less brightly.

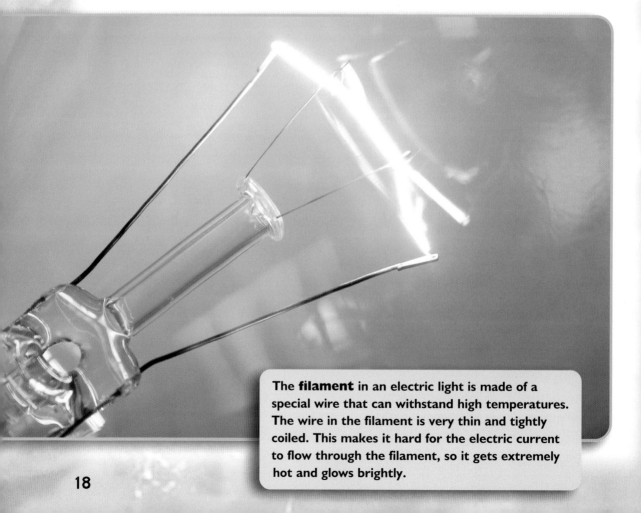

The **filament** in an electric light is made of a
special wire that can withstand high temperatures.
The wire in the filament is very thin and tightly
coiled. This makes it hard for the electric current
to flow through the filament, so it gets extremely
hot and glows brightly.

Taking measurements

As we have seen, the brightness of a light bulb can give some idea of how much electricity is flowing through a circuit. A better way is to measure the current using an instrument called an **ammeter**. The amount of current flowing through a circuit is measured in amps (A). Circuits powered by ordinary cells or batteries usually have only a small current flow, perhaps a tenth of an amp. The current through electrical devices connected to the household electricity can be much higher—30A or more.

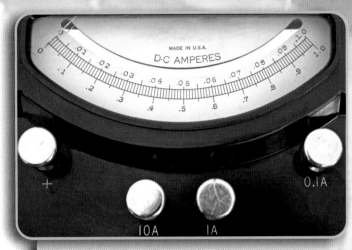

The sensitivity of this ammeter can be changed. It can measure a maximum current of 10A, 1A or 0.1A.

CURRENT, VOLTAGE AND RESISTANCE

Current
- Current is flow of electricity.
- The current is the same in the wires before and after a component.
- Current is measured in amperes, or amps (A).

Voltage
- **Voltage** is the force with which a battery or **generator** can push electricity around a circuit.
- The voltage of a particular battery is fixed.
- Adding more cells to the battery can increase the voltage.
- The higher the voltage, the more current flows through the circuit.
- Voltage is measured in volts (V).

Resistance
- Resistance is how much the components and wires in a circuit oppose the flow of electricity around it.
- The higher the resistance in a circuit, the less current flows through it.
- Resistance is measured in ohms (Ω).

Series and parallel connections

When there is more than one **component** in a circuit, they can be connected up in different ways. For instance, take a circuit with a battery and two bulbs. You could connect the bulbs in line, one after the other. This is known as **series connection**. But you could also connect one of the bulbs to the battery, and the other bulb across the terminals of the first bulb. This is called **parallel connection**.

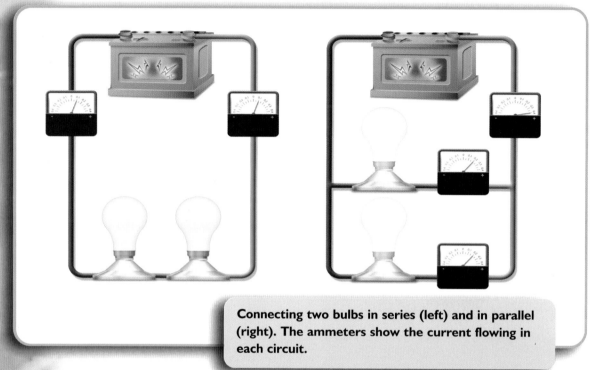

Connecting two bulbs in series (left) and in parallel (right). The ammeters show the current flowing in each circuit.

Series circuits

Let's look first at a series circuit. If we first connect one light bulb, then two light bulbs in series, we find that two bulbs glow less brightly than a single one. If we use an **ammeter** to test the current in a series circuit, we find that the current is the same all the way around. However, with two bulbs connected, the current is less than with only one bulb.

Parallel circuits

If we connect one light bulb first, then two light bulbs in parallel, the two bulbs glow as brightly as one did by itself. If we test the current in the circuit, we find that in the wires close to the battery, the current is twice as large as in the series circuit. The current divides between the two bulbs, each one getting as much current as a single bulb in a series circuit.

Connecting two bulbs in parallel seems to have advantages, but there is a drawback. When two bulbs are connected in parallel, they draw more current from the battery than one bulb does. This means that the battery runs down more quickly than in a series circuit.

Christmas lights

When lights are connected in series, if one bulb breaks, all the other lights go out. This is because the conducting path around the circuit is broken. However, strings of lights connected in series are cheaper than bulbs connected in parallel, and they use less power. So manufacturers of Christmas lights have come up with an ingenious way to use bulbs strung in series. Each bulb has an extra wire in it known as a **shunt**. If a bulb blows, the shunt wire carries electric current through the broken bulb. This allows the other lights to stay lit, because the conducting path is not broken.

Christmas tree lights are often connected in series, because bulbs connected this way are cheaper and use less power.

CHAPTER 4

Household power supply

Batteries are useful when you are on the move, but most of the electricity we use comes through the household power supply. This is produced in power stations, where oil, gas, or another kind of power is used to turn a **turbine** (an arrangement of fanlike blades around a central shaft). The spinning turbine powers an electric **generator**.

Spreading the power

Power stations produce electricity at a high **voltage**—usually about 20,000 volts. However, the electricity often has to travel long distances to where it is needed, and a great deal of power can be lost in this process. To reduce losses, the voltage of the electricity is stepped up to 500,000 volts or more using a **transformer**—a device that increases or decreases electric voltage. Sending electricity at such high voltages keeps waste to a minimum.

An electricity substation is a place where electricity is transformed from one voltage to another. The large pylon (left) brings high-voltage electricity from the power station into the substation (right), where transformers reduce the voltage.

When the high-voltage supply reaches an area where electricity is needed, the voltage is stepped down again using transformers. Homes have an electricity supply of between 110 and 240 V, depending on the country. Railroads and heavy industry use electricity at much higher voltages—tens of thousands of volts.

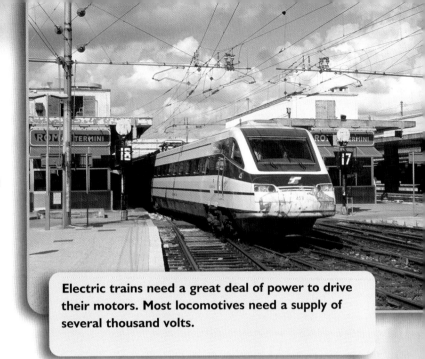

Electric trains need a great deal of power to drive their motors. Most locomotives need a supply of several thousand volts.

Changing current

A battery supplies an unchanging electric current: one end of the battery is always positive, and one is negative. This is known as **direct current** (**DC**). However, mains electricity is **alternating current** (**AC**). This means that the direction the current flows in keeps changing. In mains electricity the current changes direction 50 or 60 times per second! This is because of the way the electricity is generated (see page 34). AC works as well as DC, and it has the advantage that transformers can step the voltage up and down, allowing electricity to be transmitted efficiently over long distances.

GREAT SCIENTISTS

Swan, Edison, and Tesla

The first practical electric light bulb was developed by the Scottish scientist, Joseph Swan, in 1878, and in 1880, he gave the first large-scale demonstration of electric lights. The U.S. inventor, Thomas Edison, developed his own light bulb in 1879, and he was the first to set up a power station and start supplying electricity to homes. Edison's first power station was opened in Pearl Street, New York City, in 1882. It had six large dynamos (DC generators) that could supply enough power for 1,400 light bulbs within a mile radius. In 1885, a rival company, Westinghouse Electric, began to use AC generators designed by the inventor, Nikola Tesla. These proved to be more efficient, and within a few years they replaced dynamos. AC generators are still the standard generator used today.

Electricity at home

Look around your house and count the number of things that are powered by the household power supply. There are all the lights, large machines, such as the stove and washing machine, and smaller devices, such as televisions, computers, stereos, and tools. All of them have to be connected to the electricity supply to work. Yet only a single cable connects your house to the power grid. How does it work?

Splitting the supply

Once inside the house, the mains cable usually goes to a control box known as the **consumer unit**. In the consumer unit, the supply splits into several different circuits.

An electrician instaling the wiring in a new house. He is using an **ammeter** to check that the circuits he has set up are working correctly.

 A SAFE SUPPLY

The electricity supply to your home is powerful, and it can be dangerous. If there is a short circuit, it could cause a fire or damage the wiring in the house.

To avoid this kind of problem, the wiring usually has two built-in safeguards. Anything that is plugged into a socket has a fuse in the plug. A **fuse** is a piece of wire that is designed to be a "weak point" in the circuit. If too much current flows through the wires, the fuse blows (the wire in the fuse breaks) and breaks the circuit. As a second protection, at the consumer panel each individual circuit has its own trip switch. This is similar to a fuse, but it breaks the circuit by turning off a switch rather than breaking a wire.

There are three main types of circuit in the house. The first type of circuit is for appliances, such as the stove or washing machine, which need a high current. Each device of this kind usually has its own circuit, which can carry a current of 30 amps or more.

Next in line are the circuits that supply the sockets in each room. Often, all the sockets on one floor of the house are connected together on one circuit that can carry a current of 20 or 30 amps. The sockets are connected in **parallel**.

The third type of circuit is for supplying electricity to the lights. Each circuit usually connects all the lights on one floor. Lights use less current than other devices, so the lighting circuits only carry a current of 5 amps. Like the sockets, the lights are connected in parallel.

The power supply to your home is split into several different circuits. Electric stoves have their own separate high-**voltage** circuit.

CHAPTER 5

Magnetic attraction

Most of us take magnets for granted. We might think they are useful for sticking things on the refrigerator, but we are not aware of the many different ways that magnets are used all around us, every day. The hard disk on a computer, the seal on a fridge door, electric motors, and even the fastest train ever to carry passengers all rely on magnetism.

Magnet basics

Magnetism is a force of nature. Only a few materials are magnetic—iron, nickel, cobalt, and materials containing these substances. When one of these materials is magnetized, it attracts other magnetic materials. Every magnet has two ends, or poles—a north-seeking (north) pole and a south-seeking (south) pole. Opposite poles of two magnets attract each other, and like poles repel each other.

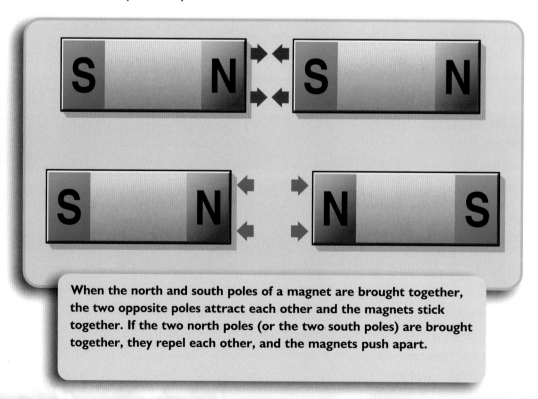

When the north and south poles of a magnet are brought together, the two opposite poles attract each other and the magnets stick together. If the two north poles (or the two south poles) are brought together, they repel each other, and the magnets push apart.

AMAZING FACTS

Fridge magnets

Fridge magnets don't seem to have a north and a south pole. One end of a fridge magnet will attract either pole of another magnet. This is because of a fridge magnet's construction. It is made up of a number of thin strip magnets laid side by side, with the north pole of one magnet next to the south pole of the next. Each end of the magnet is a series of north and south poles, so it can attract both the north and the south poles of another magnet.

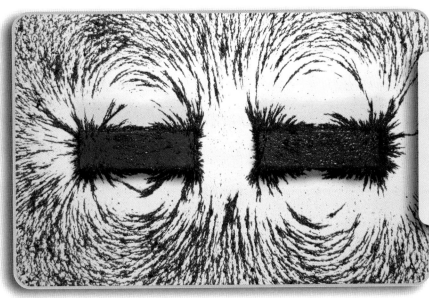

These iron filings show the invisible magnetic field around a bar magnet. Where the iron filings are bunched together, the magnetic field is stronger.

Around any magnet there is an area where its magnetic force acts. This is its magnetic field. The magnetic field is strongest at the two poles, and weakest halfway between them.

Magnetism and charge

If you look at the basics of magnetic properties, you can see that there are similarities between magnets and objects with an electric charge. Only some materials can hold an electric charge. Similarly, only some materials (but not the same ones that hold charge) can be magnetized. There are two types of charge, positive and negative. Also, there are two poles to a magnet, north and south. Charged objects of opposite charge attract each other, and the opposite poles of two magnets attract each other.

How magnetism works

Like electricity, magnetism is a property of the **atoms** that make up all materials. Each atom acts like a tiny magnet. In most materials, these atomic "magnets" point in any direction. However, in a magnetic material, groups of atoms are organized into small areas called **domains**, in which all the atomic magnets point the same way. When the material is not magnetized, the domains point in random directions and there is no overall magnetism. However, in a magnetic field, most of the domains line up, and the material becomes a magnet.

 AMAZING FACTS

Compasses

One of the most important uses of permanent magnets is in compasses. If a magnet is hung up or mounted so that it can turn freely, it always comes to rest pointing north to south. This happens because Earth itself has a magnetic field. It is as if there is a powerful bar magnet in the center of Earth, which is strong enough for the magnetic field to be felt at the surface. Compasses line up with this magnetic field, which runs north to south.

A ship's compass, set in a cylindrical stand called a binnacle. The compass is mounted in such a way that it stays level as the ship moves. The large balls on either side are magnets, which cancel out the effects of iron objects on the ship that would otherwise affect the compass.

Uses of magnets

We have already mentioned using magnets to stick things on the refrigerator. There are also strong magnets in the seal around the fridge door that hold the door closed. Magnets are also used for holding other kinds of door closed, and for holding things in engineering. For instance, some screwdrivers have a magnetic socket on the shaft that can hold different screwdriver bits.

Magnetic materials

Different magnetic materials can be very different in terms of how easily they can become magnetized and how well they keep their magnetism. Pure iron, for instance, can be magnetized very easily by placing it in a strong magnetic field. However, it cannot be used to make permanent magnets, because it loses its magnetism as soon as it is out of the magnetic field. Steel is a better material for permanent magnets. It is harder to magnetize, but once it is magnetized, it holds its magnetism even when the magnetic field is taken away.

! AMAZING FACTS

Magnetic information

Magnetism can be used to store all kinds of information. Sound and video tapes, computer hard drives, and the strips on the back of credit cards all store information as patterns of microscopic spots of magnetism on their surface.

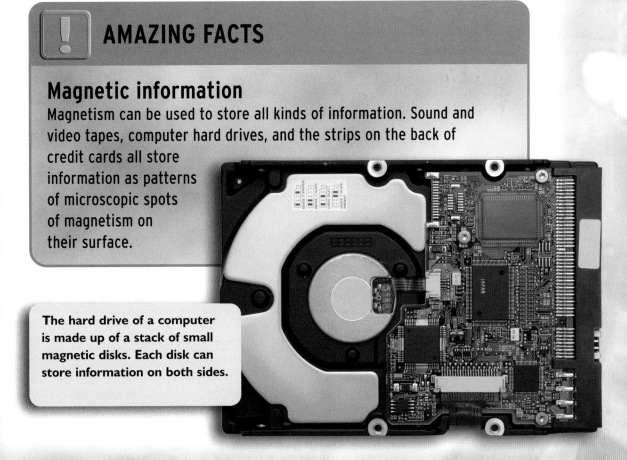

The hard drive of a computer is made up of a stack of small magnetic disks. Each disk can store information on both sides.

CHAPTER 6

Magnetic electricity

Many experiments have shown that electricity and magnetism are closely connected. A good example of this is an electromagnet. An **electromagnet** is a coil of insulated wire wrapped around a metal core. When electricity passes through the wire, the core becomes magnetized. You can make a simple electromagnet by wrapping insulated wire around a large bolt or nail. If the bolt is connected into a circuit with a battery, it will become an electromagnet.

 ## AMAZING FACTS

Levitating magnets

If two magnets are placed on top of each other with like poles facing each other, the **repulsion** between them will make the top magnet rise up, or levitate. This principle is used in maglev (magnetic levitation) trains. Magnets on the base of the train repel magnets in the track, so that the whole train floats. This greatly reduces noise and friction, and makes it possible for the trains to travel very fast. The experimental Japanese JR-maglev has travelled at speeds of up to 363 mph (581 km/h), faster than any wheeled train.

A maglev train exhibited at Munich Airport. A planned link from Munich Airport to the city center will use maglevs like this. The 23-mile (37-km) journey will take just 10 minutes.

Instant magnetism

Electromagnets have the same properties as permanent magnets, but an electromagnet can be turned on and off at the flick of a switch. It is also easy to change the polarity of an electromagnet (in other words, change the north and south poles), simply by reversing the direction of the electric current through the coil.

Both the coil of wire and the iron core affect an electromagnet's strength. Adding more coils to an electromagnet makes it stronger. A coil of wire without a core is a much weaker electromagnet than one with a core.

Uses of electromagnets

Electromagnets have many uses. For instance, cranes in a car wrecker's yard use electromagnets to pick up old cars and move them around. A permanent magnet would be no good for this job, because it would be impossible to get the cars off!

Electromagnets are also used in electric bells. When you press the bell, it turns on a circuit containing an electromagnet. The electromagnet attracts a small iron clapper, attached to a springy metal arm, and the clapper hits the bell. However, as the clapper arm moves, it also disconnects the electromagnet. The clapper is no longer attracted, and the springy arm pulls it away from the bell. This turns the electromagnet on again, the clapper hits the bell again, then the circuit breaks again. The result is that the clapper hits the bell again and again, as long as the bell is pressed.

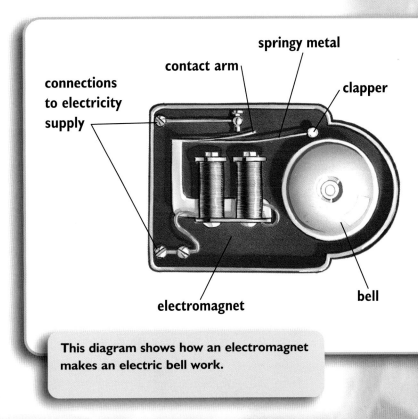

connections to electricity supply

contact arm

springy metal

clapper

electromagnet

bell

This diagram shows how an electromagnet makes an electric bell work.

The electromagnetic connection

Cranes and doorbells are fairly minor examples of how electromagnets are used. The most important uses are probably in motors and **generators**. To understand these devices, we need to look more carefully at the electromagnetic connection.

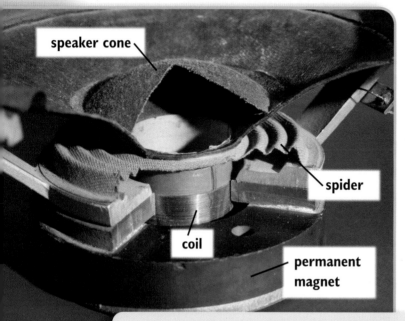

speaker cone

spider

coil

permanent magnet

Any wire with a current flowing through it has a magnetic field around it. In a straight wire, the field spreads out from the wire itself in ever-growing circles like ripples on a pond. But the magnetic field around a single wire is weak. Coiling the wire and adding an iron core, as in an electromagnet, increases the strength of the field.

A cutaway loudspeaker shows how it works. A piece of springy material called a **spider** holds an electric coil in the middle of a permanent magnet. When a current flows through the coil, it makes the coil move within the magnet. When the current changes rapidly, the coil vibrates. The coil is connected to the speaker cone, which vibrates, too. The vibrations of the cone produce sounds.

 GREAT EXPERIMENTS

Oersted's discovery

The electromagnetic connection was first discovered by the Danish scientist, Hans Christian Oersted [or Ørsted]. Oersted was a professor at the University of Copenhagen. One evening, in 1820, while he was giving a lecture on electricity, he noticed that the current flowing through an electric wire deflected (moved) the needle of a compass close to the wire. He concluded that the movement of the compass needle was caused by a magnetic field around the wire.

You can get magnetism from electricity, but does it also work the other way? Can you get electricity from magnetism? If you put a wire between the poles of a horseshoe magnet, where there is a strong magnetic field, nothing happens. But if you move the wire through the magnetic field, or move the magnet past the wire, an electric current flows along the wire.

So the electromagnetic connection works both ways. Electric charge moving through a wire (an electric current) produces a magnetic field. Conversely, a wire moving through a magnetic field (or a magnetic field moving around a wire) produces a current. These are the two principles behind the ways we generate and use most electric power.

 GREAT SCIENTISTS

Michael Faraday (1791–1867)

Most of the important practical discoveries about electromagnetism were made by the brilliant English scientist Michael Faraday. Faraday was the first to show that a moving magnet could produce an electric current in a wire. He built an apparatus in which a rotating copper disk placed between the poles of a strong magnet produced a continuous electric current. This apparatus became the basis for modern generators and electric motors.

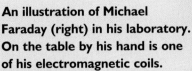
An illustration of Michael Faraday (right) in his laboratory. On the table by his hand is one of his electromagnetic coils.

Generating electricity

The simplest kind of **generator** is a single coil of wire that is made to turn between the poles of a strong magnet. The two ends of the wire coil are connected to form a circuit. Because the wire in the coil is moving continuously in a magnetic field, an electric current is produced in the circuit.

Because the coil is turning in the magnetic field rather than moving in a straight line, the current that it produces "turns," too. In a single turn of the coil, the electric current flows first one way and then the other. This means that the electricity produced by this kind of generator is continually changing direction—it is **AC** (see page 23). It is possible to avoid this change of current by using a special kind of sliding contact called a **commutator**, which swaps over the contacts once in each turn of the coil. However, as we have seen, an AC supply works as well if not better than **DC**.

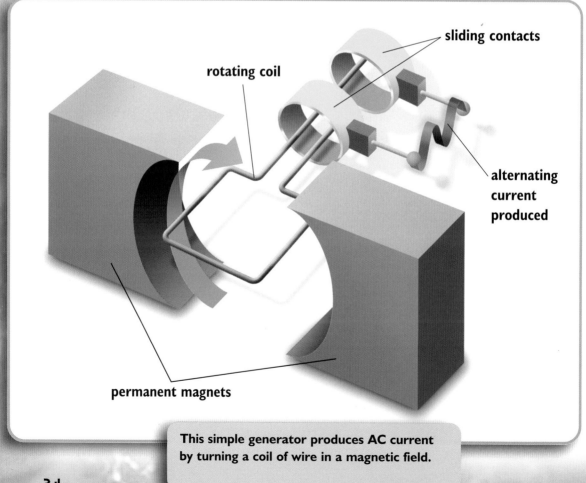

sliding contacts

rotating coil

alternating current produced

permanent magnets

This simple generator produces AC current by turning a coil of wire in a magnetic field.

Electric motors

An electric motor is basically a generator in reverse. In a motor, electric current is supplied through sliding contacts to a **rotor**—a coil that can rotate—between the poles of a permanent magnet. The current flowing through the coil produces a magnetic field around the coil. This second magnetic field interacts with the one from the permanent magnet, and the result is to give the rotor a push and start it turning.

If the rotor is supplied with AC electricity, the motor works with simple sliding contacts. However, if the motor is running from a battery, it needs a commutator to keep changing the direction of the flow of electricity.

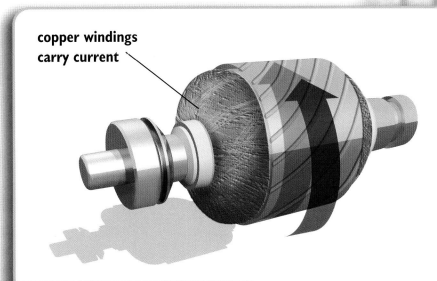

copper windings carry current

In an electric motor, the rotor (the part that spins) is usually wound with many coils of wire at different angles. This makes the rotor spin more smoothly.

 AMAZING FACTS

Mighty micromotor

In 2003, scientists in California built a tiny electric motor so small that 300 of them would fit across the width of a human hair. In 2005, the same scientists built an even smaller motor, less than half the size of the first one. This motor is incredibly powerful for its size. If it was the size of the engine in a family car, it would be over 100 million times more powerful!

CHAPTER 7

Energy for electricity

Electricity is useful because it can be turned into other forms of energy. For instance, when an electric current passes through a wire with high resistance, the wire becomes hot. You can use this heat to warm a room, cook food, or dry your hair.

Energy conversion

Electrical devices all work by converting the energy from electricity into another kind of energy. A light bulb turns electricity into light, and an electric bell or a loudspeaker turns it into sound. Many devices, such as electric heaters, toasters, stoves, and electric arc welding equipment, turn electricity into heat. Other devices, from battery-powered fans to electric locomotives, turn energy into movement.

In arc welding, the metal object to be welded and the welding tool are connected together in an electric circuit. When the welding tool is brought close to the metal, a large, hot spark jumps across the gap between them and melts the metal.

Voltage and power

The amount of energy a battery or **generator** can supply to a circuit depends on its **voltage**. A high-voltage electricity source can supply a large amount of energy, but a low-voltage source can supply just a small amount of energy. In a similar way, the voltage of a **component** connected into a circuit is an indication of how much energy it will use. Power is the rate at which energy is used or produced—the amount of energy per second or per hour. The unit of power is watts (W).

Energy losses

In any electrical device, not all the electricity is converted into "useful" energy. Some of the electrical energy is wasted, usually as heat. A conventional light bulb, for instance, gets very hot when it is turned on. All the energy that goes into heating the bulb is wasted.

The amount of electricity converted into useful energy is a measure of the efficiency of a device. Conventional light bulbs are extremely inefficient. Only about 5 percent of the electricity that goes through the bulb is transformed into light—95 percent is wasted.

How efficient?

In the past, most people did not worry about how energy-efficient electrical devices were. However, more recently people have started to look carefully at ways of saving energy. Many countries have introduced a system of labeling for electrical appliances. The labels give an idea of how energy-efficient each appliance is.

AMAZING FACTS

Energy-saving lights

Modern, "energy efficient" light bulbs are actually fluorescent lights, like the strip lights used in offices and factories. These bulbs are about 20 percent efficient, five times more efficient than a conventional bulb. A 25-watt, energy-saving bulb produces as much energy as a 100-watt conventional bulb.

Halogen spotlights are NOT energy-efficient bulbs. They produce as much heat as a conventional bulb, if not more.

Converting to electricity

To make electrical energy, we have to use energy. Energy cannot be created from nothing. Batteries produce electrical energy from chemicals. **Generators** can be turned by any kind of energy, but most often power stations use energy from fuels, such as coal, oil, or gas. The fuel is burned in a furnace, and the heat is used to heat water and turn it to steam. The steam is then fed into steam **turbines**.

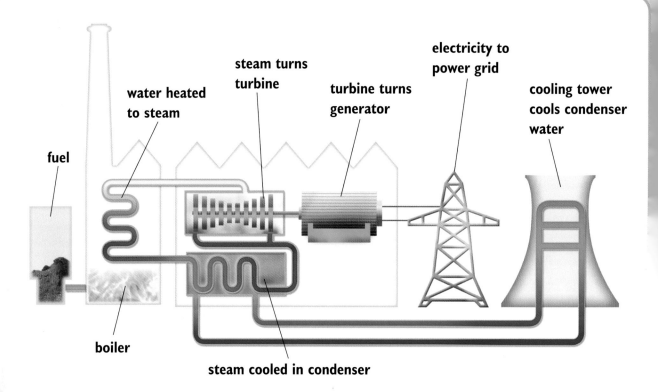

This diagram shows how water flows through a power station to make electricity. Fuels like oil, coal, or gas are used in the boiler to heat water until it becomes a jet of steam strong enough to turn a generator.

Turning the turbines

A **steam turbine** is a kind of steam engine. High-pressure steam is fed into a chamber containing a series of fanlike blades, or turbines. The steam comes in through nozzles, which fire jets of steam at the blades of the first turbine. The steam jets pass through the turbine, turning it as they go.

The steam then passes through a turbine with fixed blades. The fixed turbine changes the direction of the steam, so that it comes into the next spinning turbine at the best angle to make it spin. After passing through all the turbine blades, the steam is **condensed** back to water and returns to the furnace to be heated again.

All the spinning turbines are attached to a central shaft, which rotates at high speed. The spinning shaft is used to turn the **rotor** in the middle of an electric generator.

GREAT SCIENTISTS

Charles Parsons (1854–1931)

Charles Parsons was born in London, but he spent his childhood in Ireland. He trained as an engineer, and first had the idea for a steam turbine in 1882. By 1892, Parsons had developed a reliable turbine engine that could be used to turn a generator or to power a ship. However, there were no customers for it. He therefore built a small ship, which he called *Turbinia*, powered by a steam turbine. In 1897, a great naval review was held to celebrate Queen Victoria's 60th year as queen. As the Navy's best ships steamed past the Queen, *Turbinia* darted out and joined the review uninvited. Naval patrol boats chased it, but *Turbinia* was too fast for them. This stunt was excellent publicity for the steam turbine, and by 1899, turbine-powered naval boats were being built.

Turbinia's first sea trials in 1894 were disappointing, so Parsons refitted the ship with three propellers instead of one. The modified ship reached up to 34 knots (40 mph or 63 km/h).

Limited supplies

For many years coal, oil, and gas have been the main fuels for power stations around the world. Coal, oil, and gas are known as **fossil fuels**, because they are formed from the remains of animals and plants that lived long ago. Fossil fuels took millions of years to form. When Earth's supplies run out, it will not be possible to replace them. Scientists have therefore looked for other sources of energy that could replace fossil fuels.

Nuclear power

One of the main alternatives to using fossil fuels is to use the heat from nuclear reactors to power electricity **generators**. Many countries have nuclear power stations. In France and Belgium, over half the electricity is generated using nuclear power. However, many people fear the effects of a nuclear accident. There are also unsolved difficulties about safely storing used nuclear fuel.

Water, wind, and sun

Hydroelectric power is another type of electricity generation that is widely used. This involves containing water from a river behind a dam, and using the dammed water to turn water **turbines**. Hydroelectric power is cheap and clean, but building dams can cause great disruption to humans and to wildlife. Dams can also seriously reduce the flow of a river, which can cause problems downstream.

Wind power uses a wind turbine to catch the wind and turn a generator. Wind power is cheap to produce, but wind turbines are only effective in places where it is windy most of the time. In some places, large numbers of wind turbines are grouped together in "wind farms." Many people think that these wind farms are an eyesore.

Windmills were first used to generate electricity in 1890. Propellerlike blades were first used in 1931.

Solar panels are arrays of photoelectric cells. These are **semiconductor** devices that produce electrical energy when light falls on them. Most photovoltaic cells are only about 5 percent efficient.

Solar power uses devices called **photoelectric cells** to turn the Sun's energy into electricity. At the present time, photoelectric cells are not very efficient, so solar energy is quite expensive. Another problem is that little electricity is generated when it is cloudy or dark.

Electricity has also been generated using wave power or the power of the tides, but these kinds of electricity generation are not very widely used at the present time.

Biofuels

Another promising source of energy for electricity generation is **biofuels**. These are fuels made from various kinds of plant crops, or by fermenting plant and animal waste. Biofuels are renewable—new fuel crops can be grown each year, so there is no danger of them running out. Biofuels are used in developing countries for heating, but they are not yet widely used for generating electricity.

CHAPTER 8

Electric past and future

Electric power has only been widely used since the end of the nineteenth century, when Edison and others began building power stations. Since then there have been many developments that have made us more and more reliant on electricity.

Making life easier

Household electricity was first brought into people's homes for lighting, but it was not long before inventors found other uses for it. Electric vacuum cleaners were first sold in 1908, followed in the next few years by refrigerators, washing machines, dishwashers, dryers, and other appliances. These labor-saving inventions had a huge impact on society.

Communications and entertainment

By the end of the nineteenth century, the electric telegraph could send messages around the world. The telegraph sent messages in Morse Code, a series of dots and dashes produced by opening and closing a switch. In the early twentieth century, the

By the 1930s many homes in Europe and America had electric vacuum cleaners to make the housework easier.

telephone and the radio took over from the telegraph. By the time radio was well-established in the 1920s, early televisions were being developed. The first experimental broadcasts were made in the 1930s.

GREAT SCIENTISTS

Marconi and Fessenden

The Italian Guglielmo Marconi was the first person to develop radio. However, early radio could only send telegraph signals in Morse Code. In 1902, a U.S. electrical engineer named Reginald Fessenden worked out how to send voices and music via radio. It took four years to build the equipment, but on Christmas Eve in 1906, Fessenden made his first broadcast. Radio operators on ships in the Atlantic were astonished to hear Fessenden on their radios, reading the Bible and playing the violin.

Electronics and computers

During the World War II, early computers were developed in the U.S. and Europe. Soon after the war, the solid-state transistor was invented. Transistors and other small electronic **components** replaced large, delicate glass valves in radios, televisions, and all kinds of other electronic devices.

Transistors greatly speeded up the development of computers. But personal computers had to wait for further shrinking of electronic circuits. The first **microprocessor** on an **integrated circuit** (silicon chip) was made in 1971. By the late 1970s, several companies were producing home computers using these microprocessor chips.

The first integrated circuit (silicon chip) was made in 1958, but it took another 13 years to squeeze on enough components to make a microprocessor (the "brain" of a computer).

The Internet and beyond

New developments in communications, such as the Internet and cell phones, rely heavily on electronics and computers. We also use microprocessor chips in all kinds of other machines, from aircraft to washing machines. Even supermarket shopping involves computers and electronics. So can we keep supplying electricity to the growing number of electrical devices we are using? Will electricity supplies be able to meet the challenge?

Electric transport?

Electricity is important to us today, but it seems likely that it will become even more important in the future. One major new way that we may use electricity in the future is to power cars. Electric cars do not produce polluting exhaust gases, and they do not use fossil fuels. Car manufacturers have been experimenting with electric cars for many years, but so far, they are not as fast as conventional cars. Also, recharging the batteries is not so simple as filling up with fuel. However, in the future these problems may well be solved.

Another possible future power source for cars and many other things is fuel cells. **Fuel cells** produce electricity from chemical reactions, like a battery. A battery uses chemicals stored inside it, but a fuel cell has an external fuel supply. It can produce a lot of power quickly, like a car engine, but it is much more efficient.

Future power

Electricity generation in the future may depend more on other energy sources such as solar, wind, water power, and **biofuels**. However, there are other energy sources that could be important in the long run. Hydrogen is an excellent, clean fuel, and if scientists can solve the practical problems, we may be able to use it as our main fuel. Hydrogen can be made from water, and when it burns, it forms water again, so it is possible to make hydrogen and use it as a fuel over and over again.

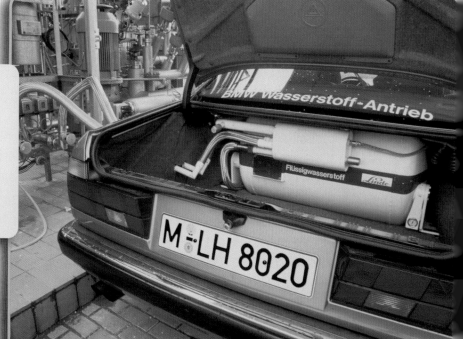

This car runs on liquid hydrogen fuel (the picture shows the fuel tank in the trunk). The experimental car, developed in Germany, is filled at a hydrogen filling station.

AMAZING FACTS

Conducting plastics

In the late 1970s, scientists discovered that it was possible to make plastics that can conduct electricity. Conducting plastics are not yet as good as metals and silicon for making wires and electronic circuits. However, they are cheap, easy to make, and flexible. Possible future uses include "smart" clothing that can change color for camouflage, newspapers made from "electronic paper," and touch-sensitive skin for robots.

LEDs (light-emitting diodes) are usually made from **semiconducting** materials such as silicon. However, new polymer LEDs or **PLEDs** are made from plastics. PLED displays give good quality pictures.

Another promising idea for the future is nuclear fusion. Fusion is a different kind of nuclear reaction from the one used in power stations today. In the fusion reaction, hydrogen atoms fuse (join) together to form **helium**, releasing huge amounts of energy. **Nuclear fusion** is the reaction that has kept the Sun shining for 5 billion years. Unlike nuclear fission, fusion does not produce large amounts of **radioactive** material, and there is much less chance of a dangerous accident. Much research is being done into nuclear fusion. If we can harness fusion power, we will have plenty of energy for the foreseeable future. However, it could be many years before a useful fusion power plant is developed.

Glossary

alkaline the opposite of acid. Chemicals such as bicarbonate of soda are alkaline.

alternating current (AC) an electrical current that flows first one way, then the other, many times per second.

ammeter an instrument for measuring the current flowing through a circuit.

atoms very tiny particles that make up all substances.

biofuels fuels similar to gasoline and diesel fuel made from plants, or from plant or animal waste.

commutator a type of sliding electrical contact, which is used in DC motors and generators.

component part.

condense turn from a gas into a liquid.

conductor a metal or other material that allows electricity to flow easily through it.

direct current (DC) an electrical current that always flows in one direction.

discharge get rid of electrical charge.

electrical cell a single "battery," with a positive electrode and a negative electrode separated by an electrolyte.

electrodes the positive and negative poles of a battery.

electrolyte a liquid or a pastelike material containing chemicals that separates the electrodes in a battery.

electrons very small, negatively charged particles that surround the nucleus of an atom.

filament the thin wire that glows brightly in an electric light bulb.

generator a device that makes electricity by turning a coil of wire in a magnetic field.

helium a light gas, similar to hydrogen but heavier.

insulator a material that does not allow electricity to pass through it.

integrated circuit an electronic circuit on a small piece of silicon about the size of a fingernail.

microprocessor an integrated circuit that contains the CPU (the "brains") of a computer.

neutron an uncharged particle that is part of the nucleus of an atom.

nuclear-powered powered by a process that involves splitting the nuclei of atoms, or joining them together.

nucleus the central part of an atom.

parallel connection in electrical components connected in parallel, each component is connected across the terminals of the other components.

photoelectric cell a device that turns light into electrical energy.

proton a positively charged particle that is part of the nucleus of an atom.

radioactive a material that is radioactive gives out invisible, high-energy radiation. Radioactivity is harmful to humans.

repulsion a force that pushes two objects away from each other.

rotor in an electric motor or generator, one or several coils of wire wound around a central pivot that can rotate.

semiconductor a material that conducts electricity poorly, but better than an insulator. Silicon is a semiconductor.

series connection electrical components connected in series are connected in line, one after the other.

transformer an electrical device that can change the voltage of an AC electrical supply.

turbine an arrangement of two or more blades around a central shaft. Turbines are usually fanlike, with many blades, or like propellers, with two or three blades.

voltage the force with which a battery or generator can "push" electricity through a circuit.

Further information

Books

Adventures with Electricity: Benjamin Franklin's Story, R.B. Corfield. Matthew Price, 2006.

Famous People, Famous Lives: Thomas Edison, Karen Wallace. Franklin Watts, 2002.

Horrible Science: Shocking Electricity, Nick Arnold. Scholastic Hippo, 2000.

The Magic School Bus and the Electric Field Trip, Joanna Cole. Scholastic USA, 1999.

Science Files: Electricity and Magnetism, Chris Oxlade. Wayland, 2005.

Science Investigations: Electricity, John Farndon. Wayland, 2006.

Web sites

Due to the changing nature of Internet links, The Rosen Publishing Group, Inc., has developed an online list of Web sites related to the subject of this book. This site is updated regularly. Please use this link to access the list: www.rosenlinks.com/ps/elec/

Index

alkaline batteries 12, 13, 14
alternating current (AC) 23, 34, 35
amber 6
ammeters 19, *19*, 20, *20*
Ampère, André-Marie 17
amps 17, 19, 25
arc welding 36, *36*
atoms 4, 5, 7, 11, 28

batteries 10, 11, 12-13, 14-21, 22, 23, 37, 38, 44
binnacles 28, *28*
biofuels 41, 44

Christmas lights 21, *21*
circuit symbols 15, *15*
circuits 14, 15, 16, 18, 19, 20, 21, 24, 25, 31, 34, 36, 37
communications 42-43
commutators 34, 35
compasses 28, *28*, 32
components 14, 15, 16, 18, 19, 20, 37
computers 15, 26, 29, *29*, 43, *43*
conducting materials 9, 11, 45
consumer units 24

direct current (DC) 23, 34

Earth's magnetic field 28
Edison, Thomas 23, 42
electric appliances 25, *25*, 36, 37, 42, *42*
electric bells 31, *31*, 36
electric cars 44, *44*
electric charge 4, 6-7, 8, 9, 10, 11, 13, 27
electric current 10, 12, 13, 14, 15, 16, 17, 19, 20, 21, 23, 24, 25, 31, 32, 33, 34, 35, 36
electric motors 26, 32, 33, 35
electric trains 23, *23*, 26, 30, *30*

electrical cell 12, 14
electromagnetic coils 33, *33*, 34
electromagnetism 5, 30-35
electrons 7, *7*, 10, 11
energy 4, 16, 36-41

Faraday, Michael 33, *33*
Fessenden, Reginald 43
fossil fuels 22, 38, 40, 44
Franklin, Benjamin 8, *8*, 9
fridge magnets 27
fuel cells 44
fuses 24

generators 19, 22, 23, 32, 33, 34-35, *34*, 37, 38, 39, 40

household power supply 16, 19, 22-25, 42
hydroelectric power 40, 44
hydrogen 44

insulators 11
Internet 43

LEDs 45
light bulbs 14, 15, 18, *18*, 19, 20, *20*, 21, *21*, 23, 25, 36, 37
lightning 4, *4*, 8, 9, *9*
lightning conductors 9, *9*
lithium batteries 12
loudspeakers *32*

maglev trains 30, *30*
magnetic fields 27, *27*, 28, 32, 33, 34, 35
magnetic metals 29
magnetic resonance imaging 5
magnetism 5, 26-35
magnets 26-27, *26*, *27*, 28, 29, 30, 33
Marconi, Guglielmo 43
MP3 players 14, *14*

nuclear power 40, 45
nuclear-powered batteries 13

Oersted, Christian 32
ohms 19

parallel connections 20-21, *20*, 25
Parsons, Charles 39
permanent magnets 28, 31, 32, 35
plasma globes 6
power stations 17, 22, 23, 38, *38*, 42

radio 42, 43
radioactivity 13, 45
rechargeable batteries 12, 13, 44
resistance 18, 19
rotors 35, *35*, 39

saving energy 37
semiconductors 13, 41
series connections 20-21, *20*
short circuits 18, 24
shunt wires 21
solar power 13, 41, *41*, 44
spacecraft 4, 13, *13*
static electricity 4, 5, 6-7, 8
Swan, Joseph 23
switches 14, 24

telegraph 42, 43
telephones 42
televisions 42, 43
Tesla, Nikola 23
Thales of Miletus 6
transformers 22, 23
turbines 22, 38-39, *38*, 40
Turbinia 39, *39*

Volta, Alessandro 10, *10*, 11
voltage 16, 17, 19, 22, 23, 25, 37
voltaic piles 10, 11, *11*, 12
Voyager I and *II* 13, *13*

watts 37
wave power 41
wind power 40, *40*, 44